In
CLASSICAL
mood

Myth & Magic

Myth & Magic

The allure of ancient myths and magical tales has fired the imagination of composers throughout the centuries. Witchcraft, sorcery, mystery and outright fear are all represented in contrasting ways in this volume. Compare the creeping terror of Mussorgsky's cannibalistic witch, Baba Yaga, with the haunting beauty of Tchaikovsky's *Swan Lake*; the vibrant exhilaration of Falla's *Ritual Fire Dance* with the eerie sensuality of Saint-Saëns's *Danse macabre*; and the dramatic excitement of Stravinsky's *Firebird* with the spellbound confusion of Dukas's *The Sorcerer's Apprentice*. Sit back and let your imagination enter a world of sound where it can seek, and sometimes find, the realms of mystery.

THE LISTENER'S GUIDE — WHAT THE SYMBOLS MEAN

THE COMPOSERS
Their lives... their loves.. their legacies...

THE MUSIC
Explanation... analysis... interpretation...

THE INSPIRATION
How works of genius came to be written

THE BACKGROUND
People, places, and events linked to the music

Contents

EDVARD GRIEG *1843–1907*

Peer Gynt Suite No. 1

OPUS 46:
IN THE HALL OF THE MOUNTAIN KING

Grotesque beasts, trolls, and other supernatural creatures abound in Scandinavian mythology. In this episode from Grieg's music to Ibsen's play *Peer Gynt*, the hero Peer Gynt is approached by wild and bizarre creatures of the Mountain King's court. Bassoon and plucked notes on the basses set the spine-chilling scene. As more instruments are introduced, the furtive footsteps of the frightening mob seem to grow into strides, until the menace is upon him. Suddenly, the music erupts, creating an atmosphere of fiendish fury. "Kill him! Kill him!" the creatures shriek at a terrified Peer.

TROLLS AND TALES

In one of his many adventures, the feckless hero Peer Gynt falls for a mysterious beauty who leads him to the kingdom of the trolls, and later bears him a grotesque baby. Trolls (*below*) are unique to Scandinavian folklore. Depicted as ugly dwarves or giants of either sex, they are said to live in caves or mountains and have the power to transform themselves into other creatures. Though trolls relish the chance to feast on human flesh, female trolls enjoy a reputation as sexual predators, and are said to force men to engage in sex with them in exchange for protection. However, trolls are a danger only at night: If exposed to the sun, they immediately turn to stone.

PRACTICAL MAN

Grieg's international acclaim brought him awards from academic institutions across the world. Although well known for his openness and lack of vanity, Grieg always eagerly accepted these honors— especially if they came in the form of medals. The reason was purely practical. During his many concert tours abroad, Grieg discovered that by placing the medals in the top layer of his trunk, he could be sure of a fast passage through customs.

KEY NOTES

Despite Grieg's worldwide popularity, there were a handful of detractors who considered his work to be too lightweight. Debussy once cruelly described his music as: "...leaving in the mouth the taste of a pink sweetie stuffed with snow."

CAMILLE SAINT-SAËNS *1835–1921*

Danse macabre

OPUS 40

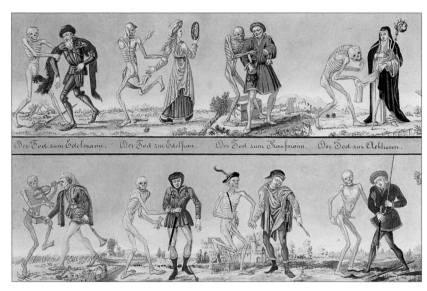

Der Tod zum Edelmann. — *Der Tod zur Edelfrau.* — *Der Tod zum Kaufmann.* — *Der Tod zur Aebtissin.*

This "Dance of Death" has a certain elegance—as if the dancers come from a genteel graveyard! The harp sounds the muted chimes of midnight, while whispering strings suggest the chill wind that heralds Death. Then Death himself tunes down his fiddle, calling the corpses from their graves. The xylophone echoes their rattling bones as they move to the strains of his seductive waltz. The main tune repeats, building to a violent whirl until the oboe's "cock-crow" announces daybreak. The fun ends, and Death slinks away.

DANCING ON A GRAVE

The origins of the gruesome *Danse macabre* can be traced back to the 13th century. The purpose of the dance is not clear, but the French word *macabre* is believed to come from the Hebrew word for a grave digger, suggesting that it may have begun as a ritual among grave diggers' trade guilds in medieval times. In early representations, Death was

shown as a skeleton leading the living to the grave (*above*). Later, the "Dance of Death" was assumed to be a dance performed only by skeletons, often playing musical instruments, and usually in graveyards.

THE PARNASSIANS

Saint-Saëns based *Danse macabre* on a poem by Henri Cazalis, in which death is depicted as a sinister fiddler. At the end of the 19th century, Cazalis was a leading member of the Parnassians—a group of anti-Romantic French poets committed to a detached and unemotional approach to poetry. Another of its leading members was Catulle Mendès (*left*) who founded the radical poetry review *Revue fantaisiste*.

KEY NOTES

In keeping with the dark humor of the *Danse macabre*, Saint-Saëns included the tune of the **Dies Irae**, *from the Latin Mass for the Dead*. Berlioz did the same in his **Symphonie fantastique**.

MANUEL DE FALLA
1876–1946

El amor brujo

(RITUAL FIRE DANCE)

Here is a dance that conjures up the drama and magical atmosphere of gypsy ritual. It is preceded by six cracked chimes on the bells, which alternate with heavy thuds from the basses as if giant, limping footsteps were approaching. Swarming cello trills create a sense of mystery, while the oboes introduce the dominant melody, twisting it like a snake before a charmer. The beat is obsessive, like the hypnotic incantations of the possessed. More instruments join in, and the pressure builds to bursting point. As the music reaches its climax, the exhausted dancer falls to the ground.

LOVE, THE MAGICIAN

Falla originally wrote *El amor brujo* (called "Love, the Magician" in English) as a combination of songs and dances, before turning it into a one-act ballet set in Andalusia. Candelas, a beautiful gypsy girl, is haunted by her dead lover's ghost, who thwarts any attempts on her part to find new love. Fearing that her spectral lover will never leave her alone, her fellow gypsies attempt to drive him away. They form a circle around a smoking cauldron, and Candelas performs the ritual fire dance to ward off the spirit. Since he will not leave her, she persuades another gypsy girl to perform the dance. The ghost is distracted by the sight of such a pretty girl, and Candelas is free at last.

NATIVE SOUNDS

As a young man, Falla studied *cante jondo*, which is a form of flamenco—the passionate song and dance of his native Andalusia (*below*). Encouraged by Debussy, who incorporated Andalusian music in his own work, Falla based *El amor brujo* on *cante jondo*. Initially criticized for not sounding "Spanish" enough, Falla's original approach soon made him the first Spanish composer in 300 years to gain world acclaim.

GIUSEPPE TARTINI *1692–1770*

Violin Sonata in G Minor

THIRD MOVEMENT (THE DEVIL'S TRILL)

According to Tartini, the mysterious trill that characterizes this movement came to him in a dream, played by the Devil himself! There is certainly a wicked playfulness in the snaking melody while, by contrast, the uncomplicated harpsichord accompaniment only serves to highlight the demonic quality of this curious piece. Although "The Devil's Trill" is easily Tartini's best known work, he never published it—some claim for fear of the Devil, whom he believed to be the sonata's true author.

8

ROMANTIC LEGEND

Giuseppe Tartini's life is the subject of many romantic legends. Born in Pirano (in modern-day Croatia) in 1692, he was entered by his parents into a monastery. After much pleading on his part, he was allowed to leave, as long as he remained a candidate for the priesthood. He went to Padua to study theology, but soon began to lead a dual life: He switched to studying law and gained a reputation as a gallant swordsman. In his early years, he was always on the move, either pursuing his musical career or fleeing the consequences of his personal life. In 1723, he fled to Prague to escape a paternity suit from his Venetian landlady. He returned to Padua three years later, and began composing in earnest. Tartini died of gangrene of the foot at age 78.

Above: *Padua, Italy, Tartini's adopted home.* Right: *Title page for a collection of Tartini's celebrated violin sonatas.*

Douze SONATES *POUR LE VIOLON DÉDIÉES à sa Excellence Il Signore G. d. Giustiniani* Par G. TARTINI *Nouvelle Edition* ... A PARIS

CARDINAL SINS

In 1710, Tartini (*left*) secretly married Elisabetta Premazore by concealing his clerical status. But the marriage was discovered, and Elisabetta's uncle, a powerful cardinal, ordered the young groom's arrest. Tartini fled from Padua to a monastery in Assisi. He spent five years there—until fate intervened. During one of the regular concerts, which he gave from behind a curtain, a gust of wind blew away his screen and he was recognized. Fortunately, the cardinal's anger had cooled and Tartini was allowed to return to his wife.

MASTER OF METHOD

After hearing the great violinist Francesco Veracini (*left*) in Venice, Tartini resolved to become even more skillful as a violinist. He tried to perfect his technique in his own way, and later claimed that he learned a great deal by listening to blind street musicians. Tartini soon became a top violinist, and students flocked to him from all over Europe. His method vastly increased the range of the violin, even though his works were designed chiefly to display his own skill. Published descriptions of Tartini's technique and approach to musical theory continued to be used by teachers—including Mozart's father, Leopold—for many years after his death.

SINISTER SALUTE

At the mention of Tartini's name, the legendary violin virtuoso Nicolò Paganini (*right*) was said to raise his hat in respect. Since he was born after Tartini's death, and never heard him play, people read sinister motives into this. Paganini's amazing skill, coupled with his dark, mesmerizing presence, fuelled stories that he was in league with the Devil. Ever the showman, Paganini never denied it. Tipping his hat to Tartini may have been a sign of respect to the composer of "The Devil's Trill"—or a salute to the Devil himself!

KEY NOTES

Each time he finished an instrumental work, Tartini played a little game with his friends. At the top of the manuscript, he wrote a short poem, often with a scurrilous or blasphemous meaning. Since many of his works were religious, the poems took the form of a special code, which his friends understood, but which the church authorities did not.

WOLFGANG AMADEUS MOZART
1756–1791

The Magic Flute

K620: OVERTURE

As a member of the secret brotherhood of Freemasons, Mozart made good use of his knowledge of the fraternity's arcane rites, which form the basis of *The Magic Flute*. This overture opens with grand chords on the brass, speaking of persons in high places and matters of great importance. However, the lively action which follows suggests a very human comedy, which is, nonetheless, mingled with an air of mystery and of things unspoken.

KEY NOTES

At one performance of The Magic Flute, Mozart decided to play the glockenspiel in the wings for fun. He delighted the audience by deliberately mistiming the notes to tease the character of Papageno, played by his friend—actor and impresario Emanuel Schikaneder.

SPECIAL COMMISSION

Mozart's penultimate opera tells the story of a magic flute that sees the hero Tamino (*below*) through a series of dangers until he attains enlightenment. It was a critical success when it opened in 1791, yet it failed to improve the fortunes of the impoverished composer, who died a year later.

11

PYOTR TCHAIKOVSKY *1840–1893*

Swan Lake

ACT II: INTRODUCTION

The curtain rises on Act II to reveal a moonlit lake. The oboe plays the mournful strains signifying the theme of the "Flight of the Swans" and a flock of swan maidens soon appears. Their leader, wearing a crown, is Princess Odette. Like her companions, she has been turned into a swan by the evil magician von Rotbart, but is able to take on human form at midnight. Tonight, she encounters Prince Siegfried, who falls in love with her. Tchaikovsky's use of glorious, ripe melodies and luscious harmonies creates a sense of romantic enchantment that has justly made this the most popular of all ballets.

BIRTH OF A SWAN

Acclaimed as one of the great ballets, *Swan Lake* was Tchaikovsky's first attempt at writing for this art form. As he said, "I accepted the work partly because I need the money, but also because I have long had the wish to try my hand at this kind of work." He first pondered the subject while staying with his sister Alexandra Davydova in 1871: A children's show was being devised for which he provided the music. Although that piece does not survive in its original form, some of the melodies may have been used for *Swan Lake*, which he finished five years later.

Tchaikovsky (center) seated alongside Alexandra Davydova and her family.

SWANS AND MYTH

Swans have long held a place in the folklore of many cultures. Greek, Celtic, Hindu, and Nordic mythology all contain tales in which humans turn into swans or the birds take on human form. *Swan Lake* was inspired by Nordic myth, as were Wagner's operatic creations, the Valkyries—helmeted goddesses on flying steeds who could turn into swan maidens. In this form, they appeared on lonely lakes, where they shed their plumage and became human. If a man stole their wings, they would be bound to him forever.

Twelve enchanted princes return to human form in the tale The Wild Swans.

KEY NOTES

Tchaikovsky died believing Swan Lake was a failure—its first performance was choreographed by an undistinguished ballet master for a lackluster ballerina. A year after the composer's death, it was revived, and went on to become the world's most popular ballet.

JOHANN SEBASTIAN BACH *1685–1750*

Toccata and Fugue in D Minor

BWV565

From its opening bars, there is drama in every note and echo of Bach's thrilling *Toccata and Fugue*. The booming resonance of the organ suggests a forbidding landscape of gothic churches, cavernous vaults, and haunted castles. As the tones of the mighty instrument descend to the depth of its register, their power reinforces the sense of brooding menace. For a time, the mood is lightened by the many themes of the fugue, heard on the higher notes. But the organ cannot hold back its power for long—the wall of somber sound returns, and the piece ends on a deep, dark chord.

TOCCATA AND FUGUE

Toccata means "touched" in Italian and refers to the technique in which the organ's keys are touched then immediately released. A *fugue* ("flight" in French) is a musical sequence in which a number of voices—or, in this case, the keyboard and pedals of the organ—play the same themes, in a specified recurring sequence.

BACH AND BUXTEHUDE

 In 1705, Bach took four weeks leave from his job as organist at Arnstadt to visit St. Mary's Church in Lübeck (*above*)—home to the great organist Dietrich Buxtehude. Bach was captivated by the splendor of the place—its 40 piece orchestra and fine choir were in sharp contrast to his own humble church. When he returned to Arnstadt, Bach confused worshippers with the sudden key changes and elaborations, which he now incorporated into his organ playing. He ignored a letter of complaint from church authorities, but the writing was on the wall: Bach knew it was time to move on, and within a year, gave in his notice.

PHANTOM OF THE OPERA

 For many, Bach's thundering organ music will always be associated with the 1925 film *The Phantom of the Opera*. Lon Chaney stars as the Phantom (*below*), a crazed opera singer who, after being disfigured by acid, hides from the world and obsessively watches a young singer from high above the stage. Eventually the Phantom snatches the girl away to his dungeon home, where he plays *Toccata and Fugue* on a great pipe organ that sits on a platform in his lair.

ORGAN MAESTRO

When Bach auditioned for the organist's post in Arnstadt, he was the first candidate to be interviewed. Normally, seven were considered before a decision was made, but 18-year-old Sebastian was hired on the spot. At that time, an organist also had to oversee the maintenance of the instrument. When repairs were being made, he would suggest new pipes and stops to suit his style. Bach enjoyed this part of the job, and was always keen to improve an organ's range. He made such an impression at one church that the parishioners paid for all his suggestions—including a set of chimes—from their own pockets.

Bach's organ at Arnstadt.

ILL WIND

As organist in the church at Arnstadt (*right*), Bach's duties included organizing the choir and church orchestra. The young composer had little patience with the incompetence and casual attitude of many of the boys in his charge. Supposedly, his relations with a bassoonist named Geyersbach once became so hostile that a conversation between them developed into a street brawl. After a rude remark about Geyersbach's playing, the bassoonist hit Bach in the face with a stick, whereupon Bach drew his sword and shredded Geyersbach's clothes.

KEY NOTES

Bach was so fond of full harmonies that he kept a stick beside him in the organ loft. When all his fingers and both feet were occupied, he put the stick in his mouth and used it to reach extra keys.

GUSTAV HOLST *1874–1934*

The Planets

URANUS, THE MAGICIAN

This movement from Holst's first large-scale work is subtitled "The Magician" because astrologers attribute an inventive and unpredictable nature to the planet Uranus. Four blasts on trumpets and trombones serve to announce a magician, ready to commence his sorcery. The drama mounts as the spells begin, and for a while, there is disorder until a march arrives to imply a certain discipline being imposed on the turbulent forces that are at play. A still, barely audible, section leads into a slow, almost timeless finale that gives the piece an other-worldly and distinctly mystical outcome.

KEY NOTES

During his years of struggle for recognition, Holst once declared that he was "fed up with music, especially my own." But when The Planets *brought him sudden success, he found that fame had its penalties, too. The pressure to prove himself with each new work led him to write bitterly to a friend, "Every artist ought to pray that he may not be a success."*

MODEST MUSSORGSKY *1839–1881*
(Orchestrated by Maurice Ravel)

Pictures at an Exhibition

THE HUT ON FOWL'S LEGS

This piece plays delightfully on childhood fears of monsters and black magic. It describes the evil witch Baba Yaga of Russian folklore and fairy tale, who lives in a hut balanced on giant fowl's legs and feeds on roasted children! From the first tempestuous chords, fear and excitement combine as panting trumpets and trombones create the nightmarish palpitations that might accompany the monster's chase. Suddenly, there is a fearful calm, with basses and bassoons suggesting an atmosphere of lurking menace. A low trill slithers down the register, broken by startled warnings from the flutes. Then, with a crash, the menace is back and the chase resumes.

RUSSIAN WITCHES

 The story of Baba Yaga is one of the most popular in Russian folklore. Peasants in the north, to while away the long evenings of endless frozen winters, entertained one another with stories of wood sprites, river nymphs, goblins and other supernatural beings. Ancient Russians saw nature as a vital force and felt a strong bond with the land. Out of this grew the figure of Mokosh, or "Moist Mother Earth," who became so ingrained in primitive Russian culture that the arrival of Christianity did little to diminish belief in her. Perhaps because of this, the antithesis of the dependable mother figure, Mokosh is the most feared villain in Russian folklore—Baba Yaga, the witch who feeds on children.

DIFFERENT ARRANGEMENTS

 Mussorgsky composed *Pictures at an Exhibition* as a piece for solo piano. It's a great challenge, but its rich and complex harmonies have prompted many composers to orchestrate it. While the most famous orchestration is by Ravel (as heard here), other versions have been produced by Sir Henry Wood and Leopold Stokowski. More recently, Russian pianist Vladimir Ashkenazy (*left*) has created an arrangement, which he has featured many times in his role as a conductor.

KEY NOTES

Anatol Lyadov (1855–1914), a lesser-known Russian composer, also wrote an orchestral piece inspired by the story of Baba Yaga. Although it is one of the few works which earned Lyadov acclaim, Mussorgsky's Baba Yaga is the one that concert-goers remember today.

PAUL DUKAS *1865–1935*

The Sorcerer's Apprentice

This colorful piece was inspired by a poem written by Goethe, the great German poet of the Enlightenment. A sorcerer tells his apprentice to fetch water from a river while he is away. Using one of his master's spells, the boy has a broom do the work, but forgets the words to end the spell and causes a flood. In desperation, the apprentice breaks the broom—only to find that he now has two, each of which fetches twice as much water! Musically, Dukas uses the unique quality of each instrument to tell the story: triangles portray dancing bubbles, violin runs suggest overflowing water, and surging horns reflect the apprentice's growing anxiety. The final bars, ending with a flourish from the orchestra, hint that all ends well.

ALWAYS A PERFECTIONIST

 Paul Dukas was born in Paris (*below*) in 1865, and by the age of 13 showed exceptional musical promise. His mother—who could have been a concert pianist had her parents not opposed it—died when Dukas was only five, and he became extremely close to his father Jules and brother Adrien. After an outstanding spell at the Paris Conservatoire, where Debussy was a close friend, Dukas became an eminent music critic. He published only a small number of his own compositions, since he refused to release those that he did not regard as his very best. Even so, his technical brilliance made him one of the leading music editors and teachers of his day. A perfectionist to the end, in his last lucid moments before his death, at the age of 70, Dukas destroyed all his unpublished manuscripts.

THE ART OF SORCERY

 Sorcery derives from the French word *sors*, which means "spell" and refers to magic made by manipulating natural forces. Sorcery was not always assumed to be evil. Until the late Middle Ages, the term was often used to describe alchemy— "seeking after the truth." Alchemists (*above*) tried to find the secrets of the universe by turning base metals into gold or silver. It was not like witchcraft: Royalty and popes all tried their hand at it.

KEY NOTES
 Dukas owes much of his popularity to Mickey Mouse—the star of the film Fantasia, *which features Dukas's music.*

IGOR STRAVINSKY *1882–1971*

The Firebird

INFERNAL DANCE

In this ballet based on a famous Russian legend, the Kashchei, an evil enchanter, casts a spell over the hero, Prince Ivan. After sparing the life of the magical Firebird while hunting, Ivan is given one of her golden feathers as a charm to ward off danger. In this scene, the Firebird comes to Ivan's rescue, leading Kashchei and his cohorts into a wild dance until they drop from exhaustion. Stravinsky's exhilarating score whips up a frenzy of screeching flutes, squawking clarinets and whinnying violins in a dance overflowing with primitive energy and magical power.

ARTISTIC RIVALRY

There was tension between Stravinsky and the librettist of *The Firebird*, Mikhail Fokine, who saw the music as merely an accompaniment to his "choreographic poem." When the ballet was performed, Stravinsky received most of the acclaim, souring relations even further.

KEY NOTES

Choreographer John Neumeier made a unique sci-fi version of The Firebird in 1970. He portrayed Prince Ivan as a white-suited spaceman and Kashchei as a robot with a T.V. screen for a face. It created a similar stir to the first production 60 years earlier.

HECTOR BERLIOZ *1803–1869*

Symphonie fantastique

DREAM OF A WITCHES' SABBATH

Berlioz provided copious programme notes for the *Symphonie fantastique*. In this movement, the hero, through an opium-induced stupor, "sees himself at a Witches' Sabbath, surrounded by a fearful crowd of spectors, sorcerers, and monsters of every kind, united for his burial." Then he hears "unearthly sounds, groans, shrieks of laughter and distant cries, to which others seem to respond!" In his paranoid delusion, even the hero's lover has turned against him. Her arrival—marked by the piercing tones of solo clarinet—is greeted by a joyful shout from the witches, who she prepares to lead in a dramatic dance. As bassoons, cellos, and double basses initiate the next stage of the ritual, the bells toll a death-knell in sinister burlesque of the hymn *Dies Irae* from the Latin Mass for the Dead.

RELUCTANT MEDICAL STUDENT

At the age of 17, Berlioz reluctantly gave in to pressure from his doctor father to study medicine in Paris. But the young student was so appalled at the sight of his first cadaver that he jumped out of the window and ran away. He returned and stayed for two unhappy years, before finally leaving to devote himself to music. Berlioz's father disapproved of the artistic and theatrical world, and his patience ran out when young Hector got into debt by funding a performance of his *Mass*. Berlioz senior came to the rescue, then promptly cut off his son's allowance, leaving the composer no choice but to boost his slender income as a teacher by joining the chorus of a vaudeville show.

A 19th-century French anatomy lesson.

INSPIRATION FROM THE MASTERS

The works of Beethoven and Shakespeare made a deep impression on Berlioz, and had a profound influence on his *Symphonie fantastique*. He was moved by Shakespeare's

grandeur, even though his first exposure to the playwright was seeing *Hamlet* (*left*) in English, a language he did not speak. It was also at this performance that he first saw Harriet Smithson, the love object in *Symphonie fantastique*. Beethoven's *Pastoral Symphony*—in which each of the five movements describes a particular emotion—gave Berlioz a model for his own symphony.

FROM WHITE TO BLACK

In the early part of the Middle Ages, many European villages had a resident witch—a so-called "white" magician who supplied herbal treatments and who might assist infertile couples or influence nature to bring abundant harvests. By the late 15th century, spurred by Church edicts against the spread of paganism, many people grew suspicious of witches. In the 16th and 17th centuries, suspicion often developed into cruel persecution. The image of the old hag on a broomstick (*left*) was born and women living alone

became easy targets for mobs intent on getting a "confession" under torture. In England, "Witch Finder General" Matthew Hopkins's witch hunt in the East Anglian area from 1645–1646 led to the death of an estimated 200 innocent women.

WINGS OF FANTASY

In his programme notes to the *Symphonie fantastique*, Berlioz describes his hero as taking a drug—presumed to be opium. Since, by Berlioz's own admission, *Symphonie fantastique* is largely autobiographical, it is possible that he had personal experience of the drug. Even so, the discipline needed to compose music makes it unlikely that Berlioz was ever actually under its influence

while writing the work. He seems to have used the hallucinations of the main character as a device to illustrate his extreme feelings through a series of larger-than-life events.

Life in an opium den.

KEY NOTES

In this movement, Berlioz instructed the violinists to play col legno—*using the wooden part of the bow.* This is to suggest the sound of skeletons dancing.

Credits & Acknowledgments

PICTURE CREDITS

Cover/Title and Contents Pages/IBC:
Images Colour Library AKG London: (Johann
Rudolf Feyerabend: The Basle Dance of Death) 4,
5(tl), (James Marshall: Tartini's Dream) 8, (Caspar
David Friedrich: Abbey in the Oakwood) 14, 16(b),
25(l), E. Lessing (Mathis Grünewald: The
Temptation of St. Anthony) 2; Bridgeman Art
Library, London/Private Collection (Dance of
Death) 5(tr), Agnew & Sons, London (Canaletto:
Padua) 9(tl); Private Collection (Franz Ferdinand
Richter: Portrait of Francesco Veracini) 10(t),
Giraudon/Musée Carnavalet (Eugen von Guerard:
Boulevard des Italiens) 21(l), Giraudon/Musée de
l'Assistance Publique, Hôpitaux de Paris (F.N.A.
Feyen-Perrin: The Anatomy Lesson)
24(t), Roy Miles Gallery, 29 Bruton Street, London
W1 (Daniel Maclise: Hamlet) 24(b); Britstock-
IFA/Bernd Ducke 7(b), 15(l); Cameron Collection:
13(r); Corbis/Everett 15(r); E.T. Archive: 3(r), 9(bl),
(Goya: The Witches' Sabbath) 23; Mary Evans
Picture Library: 3(l), 5(b), 7(t), 11(b), 19(t), 25(r);
7(b); Fine Art Photographic Library: (Henry Stacey
Marks: The Apothecary) 17; Images Colour
Library: 6, 20; Peter Kent: (After Rembrandt: The
Philosopher in his Garret) 21(r); Lebrecht
Collection: 9(tr), 10(b), 13(l), 16(t), Mike Evans
19(b); Performing Arts Library/Clive Barda 11(t);
Society for Cooperation in Russian and Soviet
Studies: 18; Reg Wilson: 12, 22.

All illustrations and symbols: John See